huff puff blow

by Susan Baker

illustrated by Joanna Stubbs

MACDONALD
345

I can blow out all the candles
on my birthday cake at once.
Can you?
I take a big breath in before I blow.

I feel my rib cage moving
when I breathe in and out.

Achoo!
It's difficult to breathe when you have a cold
because your nose gets blocked up.
'Close your mouth and blow your nose gently
into a hanky. It may help,' said Mummy.
'It's better to breathe through your nose,
instead of your mouth.
Noses have little hairs in them
which trap dirt and germs.'
'I can see the hairs in Daddy's nose,' I said.

When I have a tickly throat, I cough.
If I have a very bad cough,
Mummy gives me some medicine.
'You cough to clear your air passage.
It's like breathing out very fast and hard
through your mouth,' said Mummy.
'Sometimes I get hiccups too,' I said.
'It's like backwards coughing,' said Mummy.
'No one really knows why we do it.'

My sister sometimes makes snoring noises
when she is asleep,
especially when she's got a cold.
'You breathe all the time,
even when you are asleep,' said Daddy.
'Everyone has to breathe air
to keep their bodies alive.'

'Why do I need air?' I asked Mummy.
'Air and food work together
to give you energy.
Energy is what you need
to make your body grow
and to run around and play.'

'Where does the air go inside me?'
'As you breathe in, the air rushes down a tube
inside your throat, into your lungs,
and then into your blood.
Your blood takes the air to where it is needed.
When you're running around
it's needed in your legs.
When you have just eaten,
it's needed more in your tummy.'

'What are lungs like?' I asked.
'They are rather like two big sponges.
There is one on each side of your chest,
safe inside your rib cage,' said Daddy.
'If you squeeze a sponge under water,
you can see the air
bubbling out of the tiny holes.
When you breathe out, your lungs are squeezed
and all the air that your body hasn't used,
rushes up and out of your nose.'

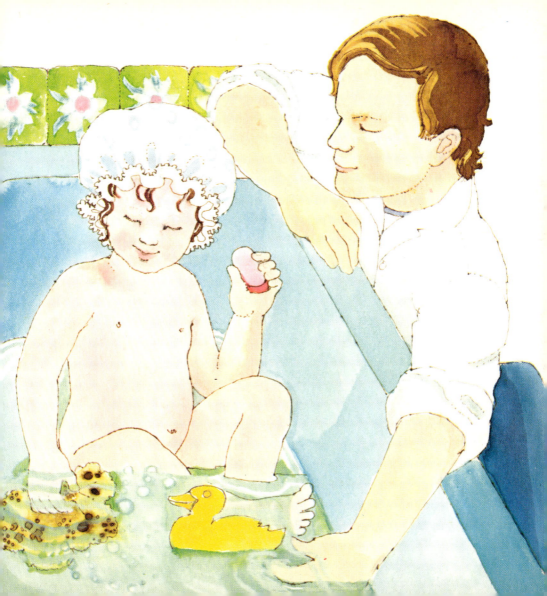

'When people suddenly have to work hard,
they start to puff and take in extra air,
to give them more energy.
If you have been running
you can feel your heart beating faster.
It's pumping your blood round
to the muscles more quickly.'

I can hear my breath when I puff.
When you talk, you use your breath
to make the sound.
If my sister is asleep
I must remember to whisper.
But when we are playing,
we laugh and shout very loudly
and Daddy says,
'Can't you play quietly?'

You can use your breath for all sorts of games.
You can blow bubbles and whirl a windmill.
Your breath is useful for
blowing on hot drinks to cool them,
or cold fingers to warm them.
On a cold day, you can even see your breath,
like steam from a kettle.
I like pretending I'm a dragon.

Notes

We rarely stop to think about breathing until our children become aware of it and catch us out with a question that needs an accurate answer. Children can feel their ribs moving when they breathe deeply, but the action of the diaphragm, which cannot be seen or felt, is harder to explain.

It is a thin sheet of muscle, fixed inside the ribs, like a floor under the lungs. When you breathe in, the diaphragm moves down, leaving room for the lungs to expand as they fill with air. When you breathe out, the diaphragm moves up, reducing the space for the lungs and the air passes out.

Teaching children to use a hanky properly and to cover their mouths when they cough, is very important, because germs are spread by tiny droplets from the nose and mouth. Do discourage hard or excessive blowing though, as this may cause blocked sinuses and painful congestion.

We have likened the lungs to sponges. Lung tissue is actually made up of tiny air sacs which have very thin walls covered with a network of fine blood vessels.

The question, 'What is air?', might crop up with some children. We use a gas called oxygen from the air. Oxygen enters the bloodstream through the walls of the air sacs and works with food to give us energy. Another gas, called carbon dioxide, is made during this process and when we breathe out, we get rid of it.

We need a constant supply of oxygen, which is why we say fresh air is good for us. Children can begin to understand from this, why we should avoid fumes and polluted air. And, while it is not a subject to dwell on, understanding about breathing can help when you give warnings against playing dangerous games with plastic bags and pillows, or when swimming.

© Macdonald & Co (Publishers) Ltd 1984

First published 1984 by
Macdonald & Co (Publishers) Ltd
Maxwell House, Worship Street
London EC2A 2EN
Member of BPCC plc

ISBN 0 356 09957 1

Consultants: Dr Iona Heath
Michele Ehrenmark
Editor: Lucille Powney
Art Agency: B. L. Kearley Ltd
Production: Rosemary Bishop

Printed and bound in Great Britain by Purnell & Sons (Book Production) Ltd.
Member of the BPCC Group, Paulton, Bristol.